Captain Quarantine
A Child's Guide to Understanding COVID-19

Disclaimer: This book does not provide medical information or advice regarding COVID-19. It is intended to provide very basic information regarding COVID-19. Please consult your medical provider and health officials for additional resources.

Are you, as a parent, feeling helpless in how to explain COVID-19 to your child? Captain Quarantine: A Child's Guide to Understanding COVID-19 will take your child on journey to understand COVID-19 through the viewpoint of another child. In a time of uncertainty, this vibrant and uplifting book empowers kids to take back control in a developmentally appropriate way. Drs. Gildar and Eller explain through the eyes of Alex, the main character, how to prevent the spread of COVID-19 as well as cope with big feelings.

Thank you to our family, friends and junior editors (Ariana, Annalisa, and Preston). You all helped to make this book possible.

Alex sits at the window and looks outside, wondering when this will be over. Schools are closed and the streets and playgrounds are empty.

Aunt Lilly said we are quarantined. That means playing with friends outside of our home is not allowed due to a virus called COVID-19, also known as Coronavirus.

"What is COVID-19?" Alex asked. Aunt Lilly answered, "Maybe we should ask our doctors."

Alex and Aunt Lilly set up video chat appointments with Dr. Hall and Dr. Gee to ask more questions. Aunt Lilly then told Alex that they would be talking to Dr. Hall, the body doctor, first.

"Hi Dr. Hall, things are so different right now. Can you tell me what COVID-19 is?" asked Alex.

Dr. Hall explained, "COVID-19 is a virus which is a bad germ that can make us sick. Germs are so tiny that you need a microscope to see them.

This is new to the world so doctors and scientists are working together to understand it. Until we understand the virus, we are asking everyone to help."

"Dr. Hall, what can I do to help?" asks Alex.
"Well, Alex that is a great question!" explained Dr. Hall.

"Hand washing is one of the most important things we can do," noted Dr. Hall. He showed Alex how he washes his hands.

"I work up some nice suds, wash between the fingers, and even scrub under the nails while singing the ABC song. This removes the germs from my hands. Now Alex, make sure you wash your hands before you eat, after the bathroom, and most of all after you sneeze or cough."

"Another thing you can do, Alex, is cover your cough," said Dr. Hall. "Like this?" asked Aunt Lilly as she and Dr. Hall covered their mouths with a bent arm. Alex yelled, "Chicken wing!" followed by a loud laugh.

Dr. Hall added, "There is another thing you can do called social distancing. This means we stay home and away from others as much as we can. If we must go out, we stay 6 feet apart. Does that make sense, Alex?"
"Yes, thanks, Dr. Hall!" exclaimed Alex.

"Well now we know how to keep our bodies safe. We should talk to a doctor about our feelings," said Aunt Lilly.
Alex and Aunt Lilly met with Dr. Gee.

Alex told Dr. Gee that they just talked about having big feelings and what COVID-19 means for all the people they love.

Dr. Gee said, "It's okay to have big feelings, but there are things we can do to help each other get through it."

Dr. Gee continued, "It's not safe to get too close to people outside our home, but we can still talk to them on the phone or video chat. This is a good way to show others we care and love them."

"We can also do deep breathing exercises," explained Dr. Gee.
Alex said, "Well I already breathe on my own! Do I really need to learn how to breathe?"

Dr. Gee laughed, "Yes, that is true, but slowing down and taking a deeper breath can help us be calm."
"I am not sure. Can you show me?" asked Alex.

"Sure! I pretend there is a balloon in my tummy, put my hand over it like this, and move the air in and out slowly. Now you try," encouraged Dr. Gee. Alex tried it and said, "I do feel a little more chill now."

"Another thing we can do is make a schedule. This way we know what comes next," noted Dr. Gee.
"Thanks, Dr. Gee, you sure helped me to understand my big feelings today!"
"You are welcome, Alex!" exclaimed Dr. Gee.

Alex looks outside the window again with a new understanding of COVID-19. While there are still a lot of questions, today Alex learned a lot of new ways to help during COVID-19. "We will conquer this!" Alex said with pride.

About the Authors

Drs. Gildar and Eller met while working together at a Community Health Center in Arizona. Their friendship has continued throughout the evolution of their professional careers. This is their first co-authored children's book.

Dr. Lyn Ashley Gildar, Psy.D. is a clinical psychologist in Phoenix, Arizona. She graduated from Alliant International University in San Francisco with a doctorate in psychology and emphasis in children and families. Dr. Gildar has experience in clinical work, teaching and consulting. Her interests include traveling, gardening, dancing, singing and spending time with her family which includes her two fur children.

Dr. Linda Eller, DO is a Family Medicine Physician in Scottsdale, Arizona. Dr. Eller graduated from A.T. Still University School of Osteopathic Medicine. Dr. Eller has experience working on medical mission trips, serving rural communities and in federally qualified healthcare centers. Her hobbies include: traveling the world with her family, cooking, hiking and spending time with her family.

About the Illustrator

Zach Eller is a designer based out of Chapel Hill, North Carolina. Eller specializes in design, video production, and web development. You can view more of his work at zachellercreative.com.

CPSIA information can be obtained
at www.ICGtesting.com
Printed in the USA
LVHW071258050920
665029LV00002BA/64